The Financially Fit Life:

Habits and Strategies for Building Wealth

By

Robert Mcmillion

Table of Contents

Chapter 4: Saving

- Differentiating between savings and investments

- Types of savings accounts

- Strategies for saving more money

Chapter 5: Investing

- Understanding the basics of investing

- Different types of investments

- Building an investment portfolio

Chapter 6: Debt Management

- Understanding and managing your debt

- Strategies for paying off debt

- Avoiding debt traps

Chapter 7: Income Generation

- Supplementing your income

- Starting a side hustle

- Leveraging your skills and talents for income

Chapter 8: Building Passive Income

- Understanding passive income

- Types of passive income streams

- Building a stream of passive income

Chapter 9: Retirement Planning

- Importance of planning for retirement

- Types of retirement plans

- How to plan for retirement

Chapter 10: Real Estate Investing

- Understanding real estate investing

- Types of real estate investments

- Building a real estate investment portfolio

Chapter 11: Entrepreneurship

- Importance of entrepreneurship

- Starting a business

- Building a successful business

Chapter 12: Financial Education

- Importance of financial education

- Types of financial education

- Building your financial education

Chapter 13: Mindset and Habits

- The importance of mindset and habits

- Habits of financially successful people

- Tips for developing a financially successful mindset

Chapter 14: Putting it All Together

- Steps for building wealth

- Recap of the book's content

- Final thoughts and encouragement to take action

Introduction

Managing money and achieving financial stability are critical aspects of leading a fulfilling life. Financial fitness refers to the state of being financially healthy and having a stable financial future. In this book, we will define financial fitness and explore the importance of building wealth.

Building wealth is not only about having money but also about having the financial freedom and flexibility to live the life you want. It means having the ability to achieve your financial goals, whether it's buying a home, starting a business, or retiring comfortably.

This book will provide you with the knowledge and tools to build your wealth and achieve financial fitness. It will cover topics such as setting financial goals, budgeting, saving, investing, debt management, income generation, building passive income, retirement planning, real estate investing, entrepreneurship, financial education, and developing the right mindset and habits.

By the end of this book, you will have a comprehensive understanding of the strategies and habits needed to build wealth and achieve financial fitness. You will be equipped to create a financial plan that works for you and to take actionable steps towards achieving your financial goals. Are you ready to take control of your financial future? Let's get started.

Chapter 2: Setting Financial Goals

Setting financial goals is an essential part of achieving financial fitness. Without specific goals, it can be challenging to make progress and build wealth. In this chapter, we will explore the importance of setting financial goals and provide you with a framework for setting SMART financial goals.

Importance of Setting Financial Goals

Setting financial goals can provide you with direction and motivation. It helps you to prioritize your spending, and it gives you a sense of control over your finances. Without specific goals, it can be challenging to make progress and build wealth.

Types of Financial Goals

There are different types of financial goals you can set, such as short-term goals, medium-term goals, and long-term goals. Short-term goals are those you can achieve within a year, such as paying off credit card debt. Medium-term goals may take between one and five years, such as saving for a down payment on a house. Long-term goals may take more than five years, such as saving for retirement.

How to Set SMART Financial Goals

SMART is an acronym that stands for Specific, Measurable, Achievable, Relevant, and Time-bound. Setting SMART financial goals can help you to achieve your objectives. Specific goals are clear and concise, such as saving $10,000 for a new car. Measurable goals have a quantifiable outcome, such as reducing your credit card debt by 50%. Achievable goals are realistic and attainable, such as saving 10% of your income each month. Relevant goals are those that align with your values and priorities. Time-bound goals have a deadline, such as saving $50,000 for a down payment on a house within three years.

Example of a SMART Financial Goal

Let's say your goal is to save for a down payment on a house. A SMART goal would be to save $50,000 within three years by saving $1,389 per month. This goal is specific, measurable, achievable, relevant, and time-bound.

Tracking Your Progress

Once you have set your financial goals, it's essential to track your progress regularly. Tracking your progress can help you to stay motivated and make adjustments if necessary. You can use various tools to track your progress, such as a budgeting app or spreadsheet.

Celebrating Your Wins

When you achieve a financial goal, it's essential to celebrate your win. Celebrating your wins can give you a sense of accomplishment and motivate you to continue working towards your other financial goals.

Adjusting Your Goals

Life is unpredictable, and circumstances can change. It's okay to adjust your financial goals if necessary. For example, if you lose your job, you may need to adjust your goals to focus on building an emergency fund instead.

Overcoming Obstacles

Achieving financial goals can be challenging, and you may encounter obstacles along the way. It's essential to identify potential obstacles and develop strategies for overcoming them. For example, if you struggle with impulse spending, you may need to develop a budget to help you stick to your financial goals.

Setting financial goals is an essential part of achieving financial fitness. By setting SMART financial goals, tracking your progress, celebrating your wins, adjusting your goals when necessary, and overcoming obstacles, you can achieve your financial objectives and build wealth over time.

Chapter 3: Budgeting

Budgeting is one of the most important tools for achieving financial fitness. It is the process of creating a plan for your money, including your income and expenses. In this chapter, we will explore the importance of budgeting, provide you with a step-by-step guide for creating a budget plan, and share tips and tricks for sticking to your budget.

Importance of Budgeting

Budgeting is essential because it provides you with a roadmap for your finances. It helps you to prioritize your spending, identify areas where you can save money, and ensure that you have enough money to cover your expenses. Budgeting also helps you to avoid overspending and accumulating debt.

Creating a Budget Plan

Creating a budget plan involves several steps. The first step is to identify your income, including your salary, bonuses, and other sources of income. The second step is to list your expenses, including fixed expenses such as rent, utilities, and car payments, and variable expenses such as groceries, entertainment, and clothing. The third step is to subtract your expenses from your income to determine your discretionary income.

Categorizing Your Expenses

Once you have listed your expenses, it's essential to categorize them. This can help you to identify areas where you can cut back on spending. Common expense categories include housing, transportation, food, entertainment, and debt repayment.

Setting Financial Goals

Budgeting can be more effective when you set financial goals. Your financial goals should be specific, measurable, and achievable. For example, you may set a goal to save $5,000 for a vacation within a year. Having specific financial goals can help you to prioritize your spending and motivate you to stick to your budget plan.

Creating a Plan for Debt Repayment

If you have debt, it's essential to create a plan for repayment. This involves listing your debts, including the amount owed and the interest rate. You can then prioritize your debts based on interest rates and create a plan for repayment.

Tips for Sticking to Your Budget

Sticking to your budget plan can be challenging, but there are several tips that can help. These include tracking your spending, automating your savings, avoiding impulse purchases, and finding ways to save money on everyday expenses.

Common Budgeting Mistakes

There are several common budgeting mistakes to avoid. These include failing to track your spending, underestimating expenses, not including savings in your budget, and not adjusting your budget as your circumstances change.

Budgeting Tools and Apps

There are several budgeting tools and apps available that can help you to create and stick to your budget plan. These include Mint, YNAB, and Personal Capital.

Creating and sticking to a budget plan is essential for achieving financial fitness. By identifying your income and expenses, categorizing your expenses, setting financial goals, creating a plan for debt repayment, and using tips and tricks for sticking to your budget, you can take control of your finances and build wealth over time.

Chapter 4: Saving

Saving is an essential part of achieving financial fitness. It involves setting aside money for emergencies, future expenses, and long-term goals. In this chapter, we will differentiate between savings and investments, explore the different types of savings accounts available, and provide strategies for saving more money.

Savings vs. Investments

Savings and investments are not the same things. Savings involve putting money aside for short-term goals or emergencies, while investments involve putting money into assets with the intention of generating a return. Savings accounts are generally low-risk, while investments carry more risk but also have the potential for higher returns.

Types of Savings Accounts

There are several types of savings accounts available, including traditional savings accounts, high-yield savings accounts, and certificates of deposit (CDs). Traditional savings accounts typically offer lower interest rates, while high-yield savings accounts offer higher interest rates but may require a higher minimum balance. CDs offer higher interest rates but require you to keep your money in the account for a specific period of time.

Benefits of Having a Savings Account

Having a savings account offers several benefits, such as providing a buffer for emergencies, helping you to achieve your financial goals, and providing a sense of financial security. It can also help you to avoid accumulating debt and reduce financial stress.

Strategies for Saving More Money

Saving more money can be challenging, but there are several strategies that can help. These include creating a budget, automating your savings, setting up automatic transfers, reducing expenses, and finding ways to increase your income.

Creating a Budget

Creating a budget can help you to identify areas where you can reduce your spending and increase your savings. By tracking your income and expenses, you can identify areas where you may be overspending and find ways to cut back.

Automating Your Savings

Automating your savings can help you to save more money without even thinking about it. You can set up automatic transfers from your checking account to your savings account, or you can use an app or program that automatically saves your spare change.

Setting Up Automatic Transfers

Setting up automatic transfers can help you to save more money by ensuring that a portion of your income goes directly into your savings account. You can set up automatic transfers to occur weekly, bi-weekly, or monthly.

Reducing Expenses

Reducing expenses can be an effective way to save more money. You can reduce expenses by cutting back on discretionary spending, finding ways to save on everyday expenses, and negotiating bills and contracts.

Saving is an essential part of achieving financial fitness. By differentiating between savings and investments, exploring the different types of savings accounts available, and using strategies for saving more money, you can build your wealth over time and achieve your financial goals.

Chapter 5: Investing

Investing is a crucial part of building long-term wealth. It involves putting your money into assets with the intention of generating a return. In this chapter, we will explore the basics of investing, the different types of investments available, and how to build an investment portfolio.

Understanding the Basics of Investing

Investing involves putting your money into assets such as stocks, bonds, mutual funds, and real estate with the expectation of generating a return. Investing carries risks, but it also has the potential for higher returns than savings accounts or CDs.

Different Types of Investments

There are several different types of investments available, including stocks, bonds, mutual funds, exchange-traded funds (ETFs), real estate, and alternative investments. Each type of investment carries its own risks and potential returns.

Stocks

Stocks are a type of investment that represents ownership in a company. Stocks carry risks, but they also have the potential for high returns. Stocks can be purchased individually or as part of a mutual fund or ETF.

Bonds

Bonds are a type of investment that represents debt. When you purchase a bond, you are essentially loaning money to a company or government. Bonds carry less risk than stocks but typically have lower returns.

Mutual Funds and ETFs

Mutual funds and ETFs are investment vehicles that allow you to invest in a diversified portfolio of stocks, bonds, or other assets. Mutual funds are actively managed, while ETFs are passively managed and typically have lower fees.

Real Estate

Real estate is a tangible asset that can be purchased as an investment. Real estate can be purchased for rental income, appreciation, or both. Real estate carries risks, but it also has the potential for high returns.

Alternative Investments

Alternative investments are investments that fall outside of traditional stocks, bonds, and real estate. These can include commodities, hedge funds, and private equity. Alternative investments carry higher risks but also have the potential for higher returns.

Building an Investment Portfolio

Building an investment portfolio involves diversifying your investments to minimize risk and maximize returns. This can involve investing in different asset classes, such as stocks, bonds, and real estate, and diversifying within each asset class.

Investing is a crucial part of building long-term wealth. By understanding the basics of investing, exploring the different types of investments available, and building an investment portfolio, you can achieve your financial goals and build your wealth over time.

Chapter 6: Debt management

Debt can be a significant obstacle to achieving financial fitness. In this chapter, we will explore the importance of understanding and managing your debt, provide strategies for paying off debt, and share tips for avoiding debt traps.

Understanding and Managing Your Debt

Understanding and managing your debt involves knowing how much you owe, the interest rates on your debts, and the terms of your loans. Managing your debt involves making regular payments and avoiding additional debt.

Strategies for Paying off Debt

One of the most effective strategies for paying off debt is the debt snowball method. This involves paying off your smallest debts first and then moving on to larger debts. Another strategy is the debt avalanche method, which involves paying off debts with the highest interest rates first.

Making Extra Payments

Making extra payments on your debt can help you to pay off your debt more quickly and save money on interest. You can make extra payments by increasing your monthly payments or making additional payments throughout the month.

Consolidating Your Debt

Consolidating your debt can help you to simplify your payments and potentially reduce your interest rates. This can involve taking out a personal loan or using a balance transfer credit card.

Seeking Professional Help

If you are struggling to manage your debt, seeking professional help can be beneficial. This can involve working with a credit counselor or a debt management company.

Avoiding Debt Traps

Avoiding debt traps is essential for achieving financial fitness. Debt traps can include high-interest credit cards, payday loans, and rent-to-own schemes. It's essential to read the terms and conditions of any loan or credit offer carefully and avoid borrowing more than you can afford to repay.

Reducing Your Expenses

Reducing your expenses can help you to free up money to pay off your debt. You can reduce your expenses by cutting back on discretionary spending, finding ways to save on everyday expenses, and negotiating bills and contracts.

Increasing Your Income

Increasing your income can also help you to pay off your debt more quickly. You can increase your income by finding a higher-paying job, starting a side hustle, or selling items you no longer need.

Managing your debt is an essential part of achieving financial fitness. By understanding and managing your debt, using strategies for paying off debt, and avoiding debt traps, you can take control of your finances and build long-term wealth.

Chapter 7: Income Generation

Generating additional income can be a powerful way to achieve financial fitness. In this chapter, we will explore ways to supplement your income, start a side hustle, and leverage your skills and talents for income.

Supplementing Your Income

Supplementing your income involves finding ways to earn additional income outside of your primary job. This can include taking on a part-time job, freelancing, or selling items you no longer need.

Starting a Side Hustle

Starting a side hustle involves turning your skills, talents, or hobbies into a business. This can include creating a product or service to sell, such as handmade goods or consulting services.

Identifying Your Skills and Talents

Identifying your skills and talents can help you to determine what type of side hustle would be a good fit for you. This can involve taking an inventory of your skills and interests and brainstorming ways to monetize them.

Creating a Business Plan

Creating a business plan can help you to clarify your goals and strategies for your side hustle. This can involve identifying your target market, determining your pricing and marketing strategies, and creating a budget.

Leveraging Online Platforms

Leveraging online platforms can help you to reach a larger audience and generate more income. This can include selling products on Etsy or Amazon, offering consulting services on Upwork or Fiverr, or creating content on YouTube or TikTok.

Growing Your Network

Growing your network can help you to find new opportunities for income generation. This can involve attending networking events, joining professional organizations, or connecting with others in your industry on social media.

Avoiding Burnout

Starting a side hustle can be demanding, and it's essential to avoid burnout. This can involve setting realistic goals, creating a schedule, and taking breaks when needed.

Managing Your Finances

Managing your finances is crucial when starting a side hustle. This can involve creating a separate bank account for your side hustle income, tracking your expenses, and setting aside money for taxes.

Generating additional income can be a powerful way to achieve financial fitness. By supplementing your income, starting a side hustle, and leveraging your skills and talents for income, you can increase your earning potential and achieve your financial goals.

Chapter 8: Building Passive Income

Building passive income can be a powerful way to achieve financial freedom. In this chapter, we will explore the concept of passive income, the different types of passive income streams, and strategies for building a stream of passive income.

Understanding Passive Income

Passive income is income that is earned without active involvement. This can include income from investments, rental properties, or online businesses. Passive income can provide a consistent stream of income without the need for active work.

Types of Passive Income Streams

There are several types of passive income streams, including rental income, dividend income, interest income, capital gains, and online businesses. Each type of passive income stream carries its own risks and potential returns.

Rental Income

Rental income involves owning rental properties and collecting rent from tenants. This can provide a consistent stream of passive income but also requires active property management and maintenance.

Dividend Income

Dividend income involves owning stocks that pay regular dividends. This can provide a consistent stream of passive income, but the value of stocks can fluctuate, and dividend payouts can be cut.

Interest Income

Interest income involves earning interest on savings accounts, CDs, or bonds. This can provide a consistent stream of passive income but typically has lower returns than other passive income streams.

Capital Gains

Capital gains involve earning income from the appreciation of assets such as stocks or real estate. This can provide a significant stream of passive income but carries risks and requires active asset management.

Online Businesses

Online businesses such as affiliate marketing, e-commerce, or digital products can provide a passive stream of income without the need for active involvement. However, building an online business requires significant upfront work and ongoing maintenance.

Building a Stream of Passive Income

Building a stream of passive income involves identifying a passive income stream that aligns with your interests and skills, investing in assets that provide passive income, or creating an online business.

Building passive income can be a powerful way to achieve financial freedom. By understanding passive income, exploring the different types of passive income streams, and building a stream of passive income, you can create a consistent stream of income without the need for active work.

Chapter 9: Retirement Planning

Planning for retirement is essential for achieving long-term financial security. In this chapter, we will explore the importance of retirement planning, the different types of retirement plans available, and strategies for planning for retirement.

Importance of Planning for Retirement

Planning for retirement is essential because it allows you to save and invest for your future, ensuring that you have enough money to support yourself when you are no longer working. Without proper retirement planning, you may face financial insecurity in your later years.

Types of Retirement Plans

There are several types of retirement plans available, including 401(k), IRA, Roth IRA, and pension plans. Each type of retirement plan has its own advantages and disadvantages.

401(k) Plans

401(k) plans are employer-sponsored retirement plans that allow employees to save for retirement through pre-tax contributions. These plans typically offer matching contributions from employers, making them a valuable retirement savings tool.

IRA Plans

IRA plans are individual retirement accounts that allow individuals to save for retirement on a tax-advantaged basis. These plans offer more flexibility than 401(k) plans but do not offer matching contributions from employers.

Roth IRA Plans

Roth IRA plans are similar to traditional IRA plans, but contributions are made with after-tax dollars. This means that withdrawals in retirement are tax-free, making them a valuable retirement savings tool for those who expect to be in a higher tax bracket in retirement.

Pension Plans

Pension plans are retirement plans that provide a guaranteed source of income in retirement. These plans are typically offered by employers, and contributions are made by both the employee and the employer.

How to Plan for Retirement

Planning for retirement involves setting retirement goals, estimating retirement expenses, and creating a retirement savings plan. This can involve calculating how much you need to save each year, choosing the right retirement plan, and managing your investments.

Retirement Planning Tools

There are several retirement planning tools available, including retirement calculators and financial planning software. These tools can help you to estimate your retirement needs and create a retirement savings plan.

Planning for retirement is essential for achieving long-term financial security. By understanding the importance of retirement planning, exploring the different types of retirement plans available, and creating a retirement savings plan, you can ensure that you have enough money to support yourself in retirement.

Chapter 10: Real Estate Investing

Real estate investing can be a powerful way to build long-term wealth. In this chapter, we will explore the concept of real estate investing, the different types of real estate investments available, and strategies for building a real estate investment portfolio.

Understanding Real Estate Investing

Real estate investing involves purchasing and managing real estate properties with the goal of generating income or appreciation. Real estate investing can provide a consistent stream of income, tax benefits, and potential long-term appreciation.

Types of Real Estate Investments

There are several types of real estate investments available, including rental properties, fix-and-flip properties, real estate investment trusts (REITs), and crowdfunding.

Rental Properties

Rental properties involve purchasing a property and renting it out to tenants. Rental properties can provide a consistent stream of income but require active management and maintenance.

Fix-and-Flip Properties

Fix-and-flip properties involve purchasing a property, renovating it, and selling it for a profit. Fix-and-flip properties can provide a significant return on investment but require significant upfront investment and active management.

Real Estate Investment Trusts (REITs)

REITs are investment vehicles that own and manage real estate properties. REITs can provide a passive stream of income and diversification but typically have lower returns than direct real estate investments.

Crowdfunding

Crowdfunding involves investing in real estate properties through online platforms. Crowdfunding can provide access to real estate investments with lower upfront costs but typically has lower returns than direct real estate investments.

Building a Real Estate Investment Portfolio

Building a real estate investment portfolio involves identifying investment goals, choosing the right type of real estate investments, and managing your investments. This can involve researching real estate markets, analyzing investment opportunities, and creating a diversified investment portfolio.

Financing Real Estate Investments

Financing real estate investments can involve using personal savings, taking out a mortgage, or using creative financing strategies such as seller financing or hard money loans.

Real estate investing can be a powerful way to build long-term wealth. By understanding real estate investing, exploring the different types of real estate investments available, and building a real estate investment portfolio, you can create a consistent stream of income and potentially achieve significant long-term appreciation.

Entrepreneurship involves starting and managing a business venture with the goal of achieving financial success. In this chapter, we will explore the importance of entrepreneurship, strategies for starting a business, and tips for building a successful business.

Importance of Entrepreneurship

Entrepreneurship is essential for creating jobs, driving innovation, and contributing to economic growth. Starting a business can provide financial independence, personal fulfillment, and the opportunity to create positive change in society.

Chapter 11: Entrepreneurship

Starting a Business

Starting a business involves identifying a business idea, conducting market research, and creating a business plan. This can involve identifying your target market, determining your pricing and marketing strategies, and creating a budget.

Conducting Market Research

Conducting market research is essential for understanding your target market and identifying potential opportunities and challenges. This can involve analyzing industry trends, surveying potential customers, and assessing the competition.

Creating a Business Plan

Creating a business plan is essential for clarifying your goals and strategies for your business. A business plan typically includes a description of your business, market analysis, marketing and sales strategies, financial projections, and an overview of your management team.

Building a Successful Business

Building a successful business involves developing a strong brand, creating a positive customer experience, and managing finances effectively. This can involve hiring the right team, developing effective marketing strategies, and creating a culture of innovation and continuous improvement.

Hiring the Right Team

Hiring the right team is essential for building a successful business. This can involve identifying the skills and qualities you need in your team members, creating a job description, and conducting effective interviews.

Developing Effective Marketing Strategies

Developing effective marketing strategies is essential for attracting and retaining customers. This can involve identifying your target market, creating a brand identity, and developing a multi-channel marketing approach.

Managing Finances Effectively

Managing finances effectively is essential for building a sustainable business. This can involve creating a budget, tracking expenses and revenue, and seeking financing when needed.

Entrepreneurship is essential for creating jobs, driving innovation, and contributing to economic growth. By understanding the importance of entrepreneurship, strategies for starting a business, and tips for building a successful business, you can create a successful business venture that provides financial independence, personal fulfillment, and the opportunity to create positive change in society.

Chapter 12: Financial Education

Financial education is essential for achieving long-term financial success. In this chapter, we will explore the importance of financial education, the different types of financial education available, and strategies for building your financial education.

Importance of Financial Education

Financial education is essential for understanding personal finance, making informed financial decisions, and achieving long-term financial goals. Without proper financial education, individuals may struggle with debt, savings, and investment decisions.

Types of Financial Education

There are several types of financial education available, including personal finance courses, books, podcasts, blogs, and financial advisors.

Personal Finance Courses

Personal finance courses can provide a structured approach to learning about personal finance. These courses may be offered by universities, community colleges, or online platforms.

Books

Books can provide a valuable source of information and guidance on personal finance topics. There are many personal finance books available, covering topics such as budgeting, saving, investing, and retirement planning.

Podcasts

Podcasts can provide a convenient and engaging way to learn about personal finance topics. There are many personal finance podcasts available, covering topics such as budgeting, investing, and financial independence.

Blogs

Blogs can provide a valuable source of information and advice on personal finance topics. There are many personal finance blogs available, covering topics such as debt reduction, saving, and investing.

Financial Advisors

Financial advisors can provide personalized advice and guidance on personal finance topics. Financial advisors may provide services such as retirement planning, investment management, and tax planning.

Building Your Financial Education

Building your financial education involves identifying your personal finance goals, exploring different types of financial education, and creating a personalized learning plan. This can involve setting financial goals, identifying your learning style, and accessing a variety of financial education resources.

Financial education is essential for achieving long-term financial success. By understanding the importance of financial education, exploring the different types of financial education available, and strategies for building your financial education, you can create a personalized learning plan that helps you achieve your financial goals.

Chapter 13: Mindset and Habits

Mindset and habits play a crucial role in achieving long-term financial success. In this chapter, we will explore the importance of mindset and habits, habits of financially successful people, and tips for developing a financially successful mindset.

The Importance of Mindset and Habits

Mindset and habits are essential for achieving long-term financial success. A positive mindset and healthy habits can help individuals make informed financial decisions, stay focused on their goals, and overcome challenges along the way.

Habits of Financially Successful People

Financially successful people often have habits that contribute to their success. These habits may include setting and tracking goals, creating a budget and sticking to it, saving regularly, investing wisely, and seeking financial education and advice.

Setting and Tracking Goals

Setting and tracking financial goals is essential for achieving long-term financial success. Financially successful people often set specific, measurable, achievable, relevant, and time-bound (SMART) goals and track their progress regularly.

Creating a Budget and Sticking to It

Creating a budget and sticking to it is essential for managing finances effectively. Financially successful people often create a budget that reflects their income, expenses, and financial goals and adjust it as needed.

Saving Regularly

Saving regularly is essential for building wealth over time. Financially successful people often prioritize saving and have a consistent saving habit, such as setting up automatic savings transfers.

Investing Wisely

Investing wisely is essential for achieving long-term financial goals. Financially successful people often have a diversified investment portfolio, regularly review their investments, and seek professional advice when needed.

Seeking Financial Education and Advice

Seeking financial education and advice is essential for making informed financial decisions. Financially successful people often prioritize financial education, read books on personal finance, and seek professional advice when making important financial decisions.

Tips for Developing a Financially Successful Mindset

Developing a financially successful mindset involves cultivating positive attitudes and habits around money. This can involve developing a growth mindset, practicing gratitude, and visualizing financial success.

Mindset and habits play a crucial role in achieving long-term financial success. By understanding the importance of mindset and habits, exploring the habits of financially successful people, and tips for developing a financially successful mindset, you can cultivate positive attitudes and habits around money and achieve your financial goals.

Chapter 14: Putting it all together

Building wealth requires a combination of knowledge, skills, and action. In this chapter, we will explore the steps for building wealth, recap the content of the book, and provide final thoughts and encouragement to take action towards achieving financial success.

Steps for Building Wealth

Building wealth involves several key steps, including setting financial goals, creating a budget, reducing debt, saving and investing regularly, seeking financial education and advice, and maintaining a positive mindset and healthy habits.

Setting Financial Goals

Setting financial goals is essential for achieving long-term financial success. Financial goals should be specific, measurable, achievable, relevant, and time-bound (SMART) and reflect your personal values and priorities.

Creating a Budget

Creating a budget is essential for managing finances effectively. A budget should reflect your income, expenses, and financial goals and be adjusted as needed.

Reducing Debt

Reducing debt is essential for building wealth over time. Strategies for reducing debt may include creating a debt repayment plan, consolidating debt, or seeking professional advice.

Saving and Investing Regularly

Saving and investing regularly is essential for achieving long-term financial goals. Strategies for saving and investing may include setting up automatic savings transfers, creating a diversified investment portfolio, and seeking professional advice.

Seeking Financial Education and Advice

Seeking financial education and advice is essential for making informed financial decisions. Strategies for seeking financial education and advice may include reading books on personal finance, attending financial education courses, and seeking advice from financial professionals.

Maintaining a Positive Mindset and Healthy Habits

Maintaining a positive mindset and healthy habits is essential for achieving long-term financial success. Strategies for maintaining a positive mindset and healthy habits may include developing a growth mindset, practicing gratitude, and visualizing financial success.

Recap of the Book's Content

Throughout this book, we have explored various topics related to personal finance, including budgeting, debt reduction, saving and investing, real estate investing, entrepreneurship, financial education, and mindset and habits.

Final Thoughts and Encouragement to Take Action

Achieving financial success requires a combination of knowledge, skills, and action. By applying the strategies and tips outlined in this book, you can take steps towards achieving your financial goals and building long-term wealth. Remember to stay focused, stay positive, and take action towards achieving your financial dreams.

www.ingramcontent.com/pod-product-compliance
Lightning Source LLC
Chambersburg PA
CBHW070800220526
45467CB00017B/540